Spoken Word

For The Living *Word*

Janee M. Reid

To my best friend and my entire heart. To the women who God birthed me to from the start The one who told me that I can be whatever I wanted to be as long as I wanted to be something to the women who told me to face my fears – to confront things. Who God allowed to shape, mold and train me up in the way I should go, who taught me all the things in life I should know. Who pushed me to strive for the best and expressed the importance of happiness. That weeping may last for a night but joy comings in the morning so even in my state of mourning I was transforming into something that I never thought that I could be but I knew that in her eyes she could see the bigger things God had planned for me. So, this on is for my mama the greatest person that I'll ever know, I love you to the moon and back so that while you're in heaven and I am still on Earth- forever- I'll let it show.

Rest in paradise Ma

Table of Contents

Introduction...

Poetry has been my passion from a very young age. It has been my solace and my outlet. From writing about my prepubescent emotions, to my rants and venting sessions as I grew older, poetry has been a large part of my life. As my life began to evolve and I took my walk with Christ more seriously -making and keeping more vows, I combined my two loves. My love of God and my love of poetry and created content that is more relatable and stands as a bridge in the gap between the natural and the spiritual. When I say a bridge in the gap, I mean helping those of us who are new to Christ or still confused about where to start. It will help them make sense or have something to relate to within the important passages.

Sometimes reading the bible becomes a bit overwhelming and we turn away from it. We stop reading thinking this has no relevance in our lives when all the stories, lessons, and messages in the book directly relate to our everyday lives. We just have to learn how to read to decipher how the messages correlate to us. We also have to allow the holy spirit to open our understanding to receive the different messages and revelation He has for us pertaining to our many seasons in life. That is the bridge in the gap, reading to understand that what happens in the spiritual realm directly affects what happens in our everyday lives.

My hope is that you read and begin to receive a better understanding of how the word relates to the world and provides instruction or direction on how to overcome obstacles. I hope it brings you an even better understanding of the emotions you have within but didn't know how to channel them, which has you feeling like you are the only one suffering. In all your getting, get an understanding for God's love; that is my hope for us all. I also hope that as you read you will even grab a bible and explore the verses that I have included in each excerpt.

Each spoken word poem is followed by a living word translation; these are my revelations received as I was writing to assist those who have not yet been able to break down or relate the word to the world. I want to encourage you to search for your own meaning as well. Even though I've provided a living word explanation, apply the passages to your own life and see what it means for you. Come up with your own living word translation and write it down in a journal to look back on as you begin to read and see where your understanding was when you started and how far you've grown at the end of the book. My biggest hope is that this opens dialog amongst all people, whether you understand it or not. Whether you say, "I read this and agree" or "I read this and here is how I feel about it". Even if you don't agree, the point is to get talking, get your thoughts out into the atmosphere to be heard and discussed amongst others who can help you flow deeper into the revelation of His word.

I pray that something within this book blesses you; that you learn something new or if you are not new to Christ that it sparks up conversations amongst the saints. I thank everyone for taking the time out to read and to join me on this journey to understanding and the connection between what we see and what we can't see. Thank you for choosing my book on your journey to understanding physical and natural and how one affects the other. I pray that God reveals Himself through the words on each page and that all receive what they need. If you need healing, I pray that as you turn the pages it's as if you are touching the hem of His garment. If you are struggling mentally, I pray that the words convict you in such a way that it steadies your mind on Him. I pray that if you feel confused, you receive the peace that surpasses all understanding and I pray that if you are unsure within your walk with Christ or are unsure if you should choose Jesus, He makes himself known to you through His word. Amen.

You had one job one simple rule and yet like a fool you didn't follow it
In your new life you took that bite and then you swallowed it
You had more than you could ever ask but that wasn't enough and your downfall is where my luck switched up
See across from me there sat a tree and there you were standing naïvely
And all it took was just a look - simple proximity
Your fate I changed just being within range of me, the tree and the possibility
Of being more than you ever thought you could be, but see
Before you ever took that bite, before I had you in my sight
I knew the time would come for this forsaken one to shoot my shot
So then I spoke to evoke that lust dying inside of your flesh to come out
That I bet you didn't even know was there so I thought was only fair that
I introduce you to me the king of the air
He gave you breath, but I did what's next and filled your ears with doubt
I knew I had you when I twisted when I twisted his words on purpose
his words you also misconstrued and that's when I felt the lust surface
The one thing you should have held dear you fumbled and I had you in my grasps when I asked
Can you not eat from any tree in the garden? That was the start of my movie that you starred in
See, your father gave you the game plan and you decided to change the course for all of man
Not just for yourself but for everyone else in your quest for knowledge
Problem is, he said everything he made was good so what's the point of knowing evil – but now you know me
That tree was the contrast between him and me
To know him was just enough but I decided to slither in and call his bluff

See he called you good and for that you should have given him all the
glory
But the true moral to this story is that I found my in
Image and likeness of him remixed with a hint of sin
Perfect embodiment
Little of him operated with a little of me perfect partnership.
And it all started with disobedience.

<u>The First Opening</u>

Living Word

Have you ever noticed that nothing is ever good enough for us? Even when God gives us more than we could ever ask for, there is still a yearning for more. Even when   He tells us, "My grace is sufficient", we test the boundaries of His love for us? We allow objects to become so alluring to us that we ditch our understanding and follow our urges. We begin to dwell in the places and situations He explicitly tells us we should stay away from. Our curiosity, our flesh, just cannot help itself.

Sometimes, just being in the wrong place at the wrong time, surrounded by the wrong influence, can drag us down the rabbit whole of wrongdoing. Just being near the wrong actions can corrupt us before we ever actually put action behind it. Our secret fleshly desires become tempted when we allow ourselves to entertain conversation or activities that are in direct opposition of God's will. It's almost like the more we know something is not good for us, the more we are drawn to it.

In the garden of Eden, Eve was just in simple proximity to the tree of the knowledge of good and evil when she got caught up in a conversation that could have been avoided. She allowed the devil to speak, she allowed him to get into her head and flip the narrative to his own. She could have avoided the entire interaction. Knowing that it wasn't God's voice or the voice of her husband, she should have already known something what was up, but because she didn't know the word herself, she replied with the wrong weapon. Knowing the word for yourself is extremely important because had she known the exact command, she could have used it as protection. Satan saw the weakness and went in for the kill. He saw the weakness in her faith in the command of God and used that weakness against her. If he can get you to doubt what you know to be true… if he can sway your mind to view a situation in his favor, he will. That is why we have to arm ourselves with the word. His mission, his one purpose is to Kill, steal and destroy. Given the chance, even the smallest window of opportunity, he will do just that. Once Satan entered Eve's mind, he was able to change or destroy the way she thought and viewed the tree. He planted the seed and Eve watered it with her own hidden desires.

The Bible says she saw the fruit was good for food, pleasant to the eyes, and desirable to make one wise she took the fruit and ate it. That part right there, "desirable to make one wise" shows that within her flesh was a desire to be more than she was created to be, just like Satan. He desired to be bigger than God; and his desire got him thrown out of heaven. So, he corrupted Eve to perpetuate the same fate. Before she even took a bite of the fruit, just from being corrupted in the mind and in proximity to the tree of knowledge good and evil, she was already affected by its power. While just in the presence of the tree she received knowledge of what she thought was "good" but was actually evil because she didn't have discernment. As mankind, just because we perceive a thing as good doesn't mean that it is. If we are using our own understanding, this is where we fail and fall short.

Before the serpent spoke to her, Eve probably looked at that tree a thousand times and did not pay it any attention because all she knew was what God told her; that she should not eat from it. She didn't have to use her own reasoning or understanding because she relied on God's word up until that point. Until her attention was corrupted by new knowledge, false knowledge, and her eyes became opened. She came into knew knowledge of what she perceived as "good" before ever taking the bite. Before the action of sin that led to the fall of man she sinned. Her mind was deceived, then her eyes were deceived which then lead to deceitful actions.

Let's connect this to our everyday lives. You have a conversation with a person about a friend you both have in common. Suddenly, this person starts to paint your mutual friend in a bad light, and you also start to see them this way. Your perspective of the mutual friend is now altered because of what you've heard. So now, when you encounter this friend, you begin to act on those emotions. You begin to treat them differently because you have a different outlook on them, without knowing if what you've heard was fact or fiction. You allow the knowledge you've learned from a third party to negate the knowledge you received from your personal relationship. You heard, then you saw, then you acted. We have to stand firm on the knowledge we gain from the source; and if it's coming from anywhere else, we have to put that on the blocked list.

Another area we can connect this to in our everyday lives, would be in your finances. It's a holiday, there are some holiday sales and you know you don't have enough to shop as you please. Someone says, "You work hard, you should treat yourself" without knowing how your bank account is setup. This is already what you wish your reality was. So, you spend more frivolously and end up hurting in the long run because you followed the voice of someone else. The voice of temptation. We have to place that voice on the block list. No more calls, no more texts, no more access.

What I noticed is that sometimes that voice is your own; it doesn't have to be an outside force. The voice of temptation, that slithering serpent, comes to fan the flames of your own desires. It brings to the forefront the lust of the flesh you didn't even know you had and that lust only places you in worst conditions. Most will say, "well we didn't know", but we knew from the beginning of time. We just decided to listen to the voice that's more appealing to our wants. The voice that gives us quick pleasures instead of longevity.

Broken Commandments
Spoken Word

Punishment - I hoped we could just skip this part
That you would have just gotten it right from the start
That you would look and see that I gave it all
But now here we are – I have to watch you fall
I must watch you work and suffer because of self.
I must pass my judgment because you didn't come to me first for help
Life – It was to be a walk in the park.
A walk in the light that I formed from the dark
But the darkness that remained played a game and you engaged
Leaving nothing recognizable – nothing the same
The wages of sin is death – and yes you're dying it spiritually,
Made wonderfully and fearfully
Forced to live life in fear of me
And what's worse – I have to shield what I created for you from you
And hope that eventually its me one day you will choose
Cast out of paradise because you were misguided.
Cast out because the evil one you sided
But my judgment is not just for you, he gets a piece of my wrath too
On his belly he Is to crawl – disarmed and defeated
Navigating through life forever beaten

<u>Broken Commandments</u>
Living Word

"I have to shield what I created for you from you", this one line out of the poem sums up the fall of man. Not only did we have it all but we were the sole cause of having it taken way. We are like children who you must continually tell not to touch something, because we don't listen. We can play with anything else in the house, literally anything else, but as soon as we are told we can't touch that one thing, something in our minds tells us, "I need to have it", "I'll try my luck"; "let's see what happens". We do everything we can to do the exact opposite of what we've been told. Then eventually, that object has to be taken away from us or taken into another room so that we can't see it or be tempted by it. We lack self-control.

It's not that God wants to take things from us, He wants us to have free reign of "the house", but there are certain things we specifically can't have because He said so. We should trust that He has our best interest at heart and follow the rules for the best results; but as children, we are so focused on what we can't have that we disregard all that we are allowed to play with. We neglect the fact that we are being shielded from some sort of hurt, harm, or danger because all we can see is our lust for the one thing we can't have which causes us to lose control. We focus so much on lack that we disregard abundance. We fall so deep into our lust and yearning for something that we disregard the consequences that come from ignoring the rules that were set. The saying we always want what we can't have is a fact!

Going back to the garden of Eden, the tree was in the middle of the garden. They had to walk past the abundance of having access to everything else to the one thing they lacked which was permission to eat from that tree. The placement of the tree in the middle to me is extremely relevant because they had to walk pass everything they were allowed to have to get to what they couldn't have. They walked past what would sustain them and their position in the garden right to what would put them in a compromising situation. They walked into the temptation zone; into what would push them out of alignment with God and onto rocky ground. Punishment was not God's choice for us, it was our choice for ourselves.

By being disobedient, by using our free will incorrectly, we trick ourselves out of our spot. He intended for us to walk in the light He created out of the darkness; it was our choice to give in to our dark nature. They stepped out of the light of the God of abundance and into the dark side of Eden where the god of lack was hiding. It led to God taking away the abundance because we couldn't handle the responsibility of having no responsibilities. We couldn't handle the responsibility of having no hardships or cares in the world.

"A gluten for punishment" is another phrase that rings true as I often see that we will take the risky path and choose the sketchy options rather than the paths we know to be true and sound. It's almost as if we can't handle the pressure of living up to the word "good" that was spoken over us from the beginning. God gave commands to all the Earth and we are the only things living that don't operate as we should. He spoke light, dry ground, plants, and animals into existence and put them in their places where they are to this day. Not humanity. We had just one rule, one restriction from the beginning, and we couldn't handle the pressure. Just listen to how this sounds and think of why we are in the troubles we are in today. If we couldn't handle one restriction, imagine 10. We are incapable of the smallest task when left to our own devices.

Just as the Earth was reborn, we must be reborn. The Bible said the Earth was void and full of darkness and God said, "Let there be light" and there was. He took what was there and remade it and called it "good". So, when we are reborn He has to take us and our old ways and remake them. He has to create in us a clean heart so that we can return back to the time when we heeded his words; to the moments before judgment fell on us. We have to be reborn into the fearfully and wonderfully made state, the state in which we find our purpose in His will, not in being misguided by our own will. We have to be reborn so that we can return to that place where we are recognizable to God because He sees himself. We need to be able to take a DNA test and the results show that He is the father; but we are not yet to that place. We are still in the place where He has to shield His glory from us because we cannot handle it. He has to shield us from what He wants to bless us with because if it's handed over too quickly, we will mismanage the gift.

We need to go back to the beginning… to this childlike state, and I keep mentioning children because many of us are spiritually childish. How many times are they told, "You can't have this or that until you're older"? As you mature and are guided by your parents, you learn life lessons. You learn in steps so you are not given more than you can handle, you learn at a manageable capacity to retain and apply certain skills. If you give a 2-year-old something as small as $100 dollars, they will lose it. They aren't in the stage of development, or the mindset to understand the value of the bill but give that same child $100 at 15-years-old and they will have the skills needed to hold on to it. Whether they spend it wisely is another question because they understand it's spending value but they don't understand that it doesn't grow on trees. Give that same child $100 at the age of 25 and they will rightly divide it because they have learned the value of a dollar in its entirety- the work it took to obtain it and the consequences of spending it frivolously. These are the stages we now have to work for. God gave us the money but we didn't understand its value. We grow a bit more and we understand the value but see how it's easily given so we misuse it because we know He will just give it right back. We are abusing our favor at this stage. Then we get to a stage where not only do we understand the value and the hard work necessary to obtain it, but also the appreciation we should exhibit for it. That had to be learned in stages according to our capacity to retain and apply lessons. God doesn't want to punish us but we are more often in places in our lives, like in the garden, when we are not mature enough to handle abundance. So, we fumble the ball.

<u>**Hide and Seek**</u>
Spoken Word

The hiding place - that's where the uglies secrets are found
That's place in our life we sweep the dirt that has us bound
The tiny hole in the wall that we tuck away our shame – out of sight out of mind
That space where we think its out of reach – hard to find
We cover our sin with sin under lock and key
But sin that's locked away hidden can never be free
Its just a ball and chain that you drag trying to find a way to balance
Consuming you daily because your soul it inhabits
Trapped in disgrace when his grace you'll find your sweet escape
To replace the weights and shake foundations awakening faith
But as long as you continue to conceal instead of reveal
No peace can be found – you'll remain unhealed
Transgression without confession brings about infection
Pointing fingers to blame others as if that will bring about redemption
But lets listen closely to the question
Where are you?
What place in life has you confined
Is it the nature of your actions or the treacherous lies
In order to be free you need to acknowledge where you've been falsehearted
Retrace you steps and begin where things took a turn – back to where it started
Out of love, your punishment wont pay the debt
But ill stop right here because you don't understand that part yet

<u>Hide and Seek</u>
Living Word

The Garden of Eden has a hold on me. As I continue to read, it's revealing more and more. Just thinking about our lives, how many times have we hidden away our dirty deeds – dirty laundry as it's called – hoping it will never see the light of day. Yet even though it's unseen, anything dirty will eventually start to smell revealing where it's been hidden. We can shove it into corners or hide it in closets; but eventually, the smell will start to make people question our cleanliness.

Thinking of Adam and Eve in the garden… just after they ate the fruit, their eyes were opened. They realized they were naked, felt shame, created clothes to cover themselves out of fig leaves, and hid from the voice of God. The initial act of sin caused a downwards spiral. Once their eyes were opened, they experienced that of lack of discernment we talked about earlier. They perceived that their nakedness was shameful but if God created you naked and said it was good then it is good. The deception from the beginning lead to continual deception as their eyes continued to deceive them into perceiving God's work, His creation as shameful.

In the world today, the epidemic of plastic surgery has folk altering the way they were born- the way they were made, as if it's shameful. As if it's something that needs to be recreated. Then they must cover up what they perceive as shame with more shame as they create coverings and hide themselves from the presence of God. How do you create your own covering and hide from the presence of the only one that can cover you? How do we sin and believe that it is unseen? How do we trick ourselves into thinking that not only are our transgression unseen but that we can create our own covering to hide it? We like to believe that the actions in the garden are unfamiliar or unlikely to happen today but we are still actively hiding in plain sight, deceiving ourselves into believing we are unseen. Believing that we are out of the sight of God just because we dress our best on Sunday. He knows that we run home, change, and hit the streets, we cannot hide from eyes that never leave us. We are only fooling ourselves. Then when our secrets are found out, we begin the blame game. It's everyone's fault but our own. Like Adam in the garden when he said, "The woman you gave me handed me the apple". Or Eve when she said, "The serpent in the garden deceived me". They both lacked ownership.

Proverbs 28:13 says, "whoever covers his sin will not prosper but whoever confesses and forsakes will have mercy". The question, "where are you" was deeper than just their physical location. Where are you spiritually? Where are you mentally? Where are you in obedience? Where are you in Me? Where are you in truth? Since you have the knowledge of good and evil, where are you in your discernment? If you know good from evil which, will you choose? Right or wrong? This is the question that we struggle with today. We, like Adam and Eve, create our own right and wrong because we are operating in our own understanding. Your own understanding will have you trying to save you all the time instead of throwing yourself at the mercy of the judge because only His verdict matters.

<u>**I Said You Would Wake It … Not The Boat**</u>
Spoken Word

As I sit and think of all the times I've lost it all
Of all the times I've been stripped and allowed to fall
I think if you promised me greatness and success
Well why am I falling deeper and deeper into distress
Why is it that time after time
Why is it that every time I begin to climb
The path gets slippery and I start to miss
Each step I take feels like I lost my grip
Like a house on fire I start to panic
Start reaching and grabbing onto all the things I can manage
Holding on to this stuff because you gave it to me
Holding on to each lesson because it how I came to be
Until in my falling my eyes became clear
I'm falling and I placed myself here
I'm falling because I'm holding onto things I hold dear
This stuff, all this stuff that's weighing me down
And I only realize it moments before I hit the ground
These things were extra – but I'm holding to tight
Thee things became me and I lost my light
I lost the meaning and gave it my own reason – the lies that I believe
And took these things into each season and placed myself in captivity
And used "seek the kingdom of heaven and all these things will be added"
But what added can be subtracted if mismanaged
And while you saved me all my things were destroyed
All the things I've enjoyed
Taken because they became like an idol
Take because in that my life – it spiraled
My life was left – it was the only thing that remained afloat
Because you promised I would make it – not the boat.

I Said You Would Wake It ... Not The Boat
Living Word

We enter many seasons in our lives where we find ourselves caught between holding on and letting go. In holding on, you feel like you're saving a part of yourself. You feel like you're grabbing hold of your identity. You believe wholehearted that it's yours to keep because if God gave it to you why would He forcefully remove it. Why would God give you the desires of your heart? Why would He fill your life with all that you enjoy just to remove it in such a dramatic way? I want you to think to yourself is it dramatic or has He been calling you to let go for some time? Has He been trying to get your attention while these things you hold dear have a hold on you?

We tend to place so much power over the things in our lives and forget that He gave them to us. We forget that just as quickly as He gave them, He can take them away. We begin to treasure the things of this world and forget that it is written in Matthew 6:19-21, "Do not store up for yourselves treasures on earth, where moths and vermin destroy, and where thieves break in and steal. But store up for yourselves treasures in heaven. For where your treasure is, there your heart will be also." We find ourselves so focused on storing up items, memories, and people that we don't even realize we are making idols. We place value on what we have instead of who gave them to us. We praise the items and forget to praise the One that made having them possible. We get so caught up in the blessing that we spend our time serving the blessing instead of the blesser. Even our prayers reveal the level we place God; we praise him more for being the gift giver instead of the gift Himself. We have become accustomed to idolizing the gift and not the gift giver and praising the temporary enjoyment instead of the everlasting. Whoever loves the world then God is not in them.

Yes, He provides us with certain luxuries but He said He would save you and not the boat. The boat is anything you place ahead of God. In Acts chapter 27 verse 22, Apostle Paul spoke to the men and told them to keep their courage. "None of you will lose your life, only the ship will be destroyed." God is saying to us, "Only the vehicle that you are placing all your trust in will be destroyed and I am destroying it because you placed your hope in this vehicle ahead of Me. Placing your trust in this boat instead of using me as your life preserver. When things go wrong, you're in a state of panic because of the storm. You see the hope in this boat is running out, so cast your cares on me. I am the only one who can bring you through and bring you out… despite your disobedience."

We have to understand that God is the source of the resources. In other words, He is the One who can provide the supply or strategy needed in all circumstances. 2 Philippians 4:19 says, "He will meet all your needs according to the riches of His glory." So, If you place your heart with this ship, you will go down with it; but if you place your heart with Him then life is your portion.

<u>Asleep In The Garden, Awake In The Tides</u>
Spoken Word

Why would he sleep in discord and labor in a place of peace?
Then I think – things aren't always as they appear to be
So I pray and seek his face for answers
That's when I heard – I react in a different manner
If I'm asleep in a storm – then while I'm at rest
I commission the wind and the waves to war against
That which goes to great lengths to torment
See the wind and the storm was caused by me
Let me open your insight and close your natural eye so you can see
My flesh might be asleep – but my spirit – hoovers over the face of deep
In the beginning
When there was darkness and void
I destroy and employed
Everything I spoke to take form
And I rested in Eden – no sleep for me either
Because only I could protect it from the great deceiver
In gethsemane I brought people with me for back up
But they act up
Showing up for work with a half cup
Fainted by sleep touched by lust
See – in the peace of the garden – slithering through the grass and the
dust
He scavenges – roaring lion sound – when we feel untouched
So I must stay up – standing in the gap
For when he attacks and darkness starts filling your gaps
Falling into those set traps
Because your living in a state too relaxed
Living in a state that's unmatched
For spiritual warfare attacks

Child – use your discernment
And stop assuming that serpent
Isn't working – because your calm – void of burden
And get hurt when
He catches you by surprise
And just remember - when he wraps you up tangled in his vines
When you look death down the barrel dead in his eyes
Because in slacking he finds
You asleep in the garden instead of awake in the tides.

Asleep In The Garden, Awake In The Tides
Living Word

In the story in Matthew 28 when Jesus is asleep in the boat as it was being thrown around in the storm, the disciples wake Him in fear. They wake Him because they can't understand how He could be sleeping when there is chaos all around Him. They are all awakened and look at the situation that they are in but don't even realize that the One who would save is there with them. The overlooked the fact that if he is at peace they should be as well. They overlooked the fact that if there was an urgent need, the Savior would wake up because His sheep need saving. They overlooked the fact the when He wasn't present with them in the physical, He still made a way for them and their ancestors. So why, being made flesh, would this be any different? They overlooked the fact that He Himself was in the storm. He made all that there is to be in this world including the very storm that He was in and still they asked, "What manner of man is this that even the wind and the waves obey Him?

This poem was inspired by that very line, "what manner of man is this that even the wind and the waves obey Him?" Looking at it from this perspective, if He is asleep in the storm why wouldn't they understand that He had created the storm? Why wouldn't He, being all knowing, remain a sleep-in danger? The more compelling question is, why would they panic if they were with Him?

Now, thinking on the garden of Gethsemane, He was awake when the disciples kept slipping into sleep. The Disciples were lulled to bed by the illusion of peace, yet He was awake warring. Not only was He awake, but He commissioned them to pray. He gave an order and they disobeyed, falling subject to their own urges to sleep. Jesus said His soul was overwhelmed to the point of death and to stay awake, yet they slept. The discernment was off in these two instances amongst the disciples because they only expected or acknowledged danger and peace when it was clear and present and when it was blatant and obvious. They followed the discernment of the flesh in both the boat and the garden. One out of fear and the other out of comfort. These actions showed that they didn't trust God's Judgement. Had they rested in the chaos, that would show they trusted that no matter what the situation looks like, God is in control. It would have shown complete faith in Him and even though they didn't understand why He was resting, whatever He was doing they knew he had them and that situation covered. Or that even if where they were was clearly a place of peace, they trusted that He would not advise them to remain alert for no reason. They should have known to fight their flesh because even though they were unsure of why He was asking them to remain awake while the others slept. They should have trusted that it was for a larger purpose and prayed that they wouldn't fall into temptation.

The Bible says, "My ways are not your ways." So, when He rested in a storm, could it not be that He entrusted the storm to cover him? He uses water in the Bible to save, deliver, and set free on many different occasions. Why would this be any different?

Before the garden of Eden came to be, the Bible tells us that God hoovered over the face of the deep. So, if the deep in fact has a face, why wouldn't it know His and begin to protect Him as He rested in the boat? If He labored in what seemed to be a peaceful garden in the beginning, taking no rest until His work was done and He saw it as good, that would suggest that there were forces and powers He needed to come against Himself. The earth was void and full of darkness, that is something only the Trinity can contend with. In the garden of Gethsemane, He prayed so earnestly that He began to sweat droplets of blood. This is indication of a war that had to be handled while He remained awake and alert. It was a situation the wind and the waves couldn't handle on His behalf. It was a situation where He just requested that two or three gathered; and in human true nature, we could never amount to the intervention of the Divine. This further proves that as we lack discernment, we not only put ourselves at risk but others as well.

We look at a situation and it seems to be peaceful but that person could be getting tormented in their mind and we would never know because man only looks at the outer appearance. We need to pray as earnestly as Jesus and seek our Father for direction because peace doesn't always come in a peaceful package and war doesn't always come in a package of destruction.

<u>Peaks and Valleys</u>
Spoken Word

Every mountain is followed by a valley
and every valley followed by a mountain
but what does that mean?
every height is followed by a fall
 but their fall is not what it seems
because up ahead is another height
higher than the last waiting for us to climb it
because that blessing is just within your grasp
but we see the valley and focus on how far it stretches
we focus on the bumps the rocks the many trenches
and we look back and that's where we start to lack
we long for what we had and become fixated
because back was a time where we thought we made it
but just beyond the valley beyond the struggle are higher heights
beyond the darkness beyond the trials and beyond the sleepless nights
 is a destiny a what's next for me a be all I could be
green pastures beyond what the eyes can see
but we have to get there break through to the other side
push through and meet the new you that abides
Yeah though I walk through the valley of the shadow of death I will fear
no evil for thou art with me
and if you are with me in this valley I already have the victory
be aware of the shadow but don't become its victim become wisdom
use the valley as a sharpening tool to sharpen you
 use it as a battleground because what's to be found
are green pastures waiting to be plowed
so don't lose hope when all hope seems to be lost
because in Christ what's lost at a cost is always found at none - what do
you mean?

the cost of salvation was paid on the cross to spare us from eternal
damnation
Slate clean, check paid and written by the son

This is reminder to all those who thought they had it all, who rested in God's favor but were uprooted and placed in a situation that seems unfavorable. This is for those who felt they had won until the flood came in and wash it all away. What happens in a flood? You might say it causes destruction but, in all actuality, it's forcing you to a higher level. On your journey to higher ground, you immediately become discouraged because of how far away it seems. It leaves you thinking just the other day, I was in a place of peace, a place of stillness and comfort; now I have a journey ahead. I want to serve notice that when you get that feeling of contentment in your position on what you think is you peak, get ready for your valley. Get ready to be removed from that place you've outgrown. It means it's time for new challenges and bigger things. It's time for you to grow again.

The uprooting is necessary for elevation into the you that God knows from the you that you see. The Bible says, "Before He formed us, He knew us" and it also says, "push towards the mark for the prize of the high calling of God". I'll put that into context. We need breaks and resting periods. As mankind, we are never in a state of constant work. We have lunch breaks, we take naps, we have leisure time, we are even given an allotted a time for sleep at night. God knew we would need that rest and relaxation before the journey. It's called a grace period when you can feel that break from the burden for a period of time to catch your breath. In that resting season, there is no battle, just calmness. It's that breakeven point in life when things aren't getting any worse or any better. It's your comfort zone. He knew us well enough to know that within each of us, He has to work in stages. If He took us straight to the highest mark, we would never make it in one shot.

Like the Israelites, He took them on a 40-year journey that could have taken 11 days; but if they knew all they had to endure, they would have complained all the more and even turned back remaining stuck. This is why God moves in increments, little by little, height by height, tackling one valley that led to one mountain at a time. So, when a flood comes in keep this in mind, everything is getting wet. There's no more stillness, no more comfort.

The Bible says, "I knows the plans that I have for you, plans to prosper you and for you to have an expected end". We expect to end at the high calling but we don't know the plans; that's above our level of understanding. We don't know if those plans are to take us through 10 valleys or 10,000. All we know is that there is in fact a higher peak ahead of a way of escape. When you get into these valley seasons, in the places where you feel like turning and going back, just think, if I turn back I will have walked through the same obstacles twice on purpose. I would be putting myself through the hardships again just because I don't want to face whatever new ones may lie ahead. I am pushing against the flood that's rushing in when I should let go and let God. I'm still holding on to what was.

As mankind, we tend to spend so much time longing for what was instead of getting to what is. New can be frightening but I'll ask you this. If you made it half way, why not set your mind on the saying "the only way out is through"? Don't fear the valley because it's full of shadows; don't stop midway, curl up in a ball and wait for a rescue team because the rescue site is at the top of the next mountain. If you want to be saved from your current conditions, you have to take the necessary steps and that is both literally and figuratively.

If you were abandoned on the side of the road with no town for miles, you wouldn't sit there as if all hope is lost. You would take physical steps to make it to the next town, right? The same applies to the spiritual. That is why it's called a spiritual journey, because you are supposed to be going somewhere. Most valleys are low places set in between two mountains with a narrow river running through it; follow the river that's where life is. A river in a valley is your indication of hope. It's a symbol of hope that not only has God walked this valley before us and defeated the shadow of death that wants to overtake us, but He's also prepared your place at the end of it. All you have to do is press towards the mark and make it to your expected end. You just have to survive the battle and you can't survive a battle you never enter. How do you win a war if you don't fight in it? Running from a battle is forfeit, so continue to all that's ahead. The past is the past, you'll never see it again so why not see this valley through?

A lot of times, we see the valley as place of isolation, where you're abandoned, but you are never alone. From people, yes your separated from people, but it's necessary for your walk with God. Use those ridged moments to sharpen you because when you reach the top of your next mountain, you'll come out stronger than you went in. Iron sharpens iron, that's what tough situations are for. If it were always smooth sailing, how would you ever sharpen the image of you to match what God sees? The valley puts you in a position to rely on Him, to literally look to the hills from which comes your help.

Jesus tells us not to forget Lot's wife who was fleeing from the destruction of Sodom and Gomorrah looked back and turned into a pillar of salt. She looked back and got stuck between what she was leaving and where she was going. Her connection to the things of the past was so strong that she entrapped herself between old things that passed away and the new things that she was running to. This caused her to turn into a pillar of salt, calcified salt, stuck in the same position, in the same place. She lost forward motion. She got stuck in a moment she was supposed to just pass through. The pillar of salt is profound to me because we are called the salt of the Earth. So, as we go, we are supposed to do what salt does, flavor the Earth. Spread the good news as w pass through, leaving behind an aroma pleasing to God so flavorful that His people hear His voice and follow it.

Isn't it like Satan to have us to turn back? Isn't it like him cause us to turn into a pilar of salt and twist our lives into a state of stagnation so the very thing we were called to do, the very salt we are called to spread, is stuck with us because we won't move. If the valley wasn't necessary in the development of who we are to be, God wouldn't walk with us through it.

<u>Triggered</u>
Spoken Word

The Bible says no weapon formed against me shall prosper so we know
that to be true
But what if the weapon that keeps forming against you - is you?
We hold ourselves in such high regard but we need to reconsider
We have to be the weapons if we keep on getting triggered
We have to be the reasons our flesh keeps getting weaker
We have to be the openings for the devil to continue to use us as speaker
We have to be our downfalls because of the choices that we make
We have to be the reasons behind our countless mistakes
We have to be the reason we fill our emptiness with dysfunction
We have to be the reason – in our life - the devil gets the first
introduction
We have to be the reason we close our ears to the real
The Bible says for those who have an ear let them hear
But if they're closed how do you deal?
So it has to be us - we have to be the weapon
Allowing the lust of the flesh to step in
Allowing the pride of life to entice
Allowing the lust of the eye to lead and guide
Then turning around blaming others blaming the darkness
To my understanding we have a choice now who do you trust in?
I've never heard of God's promises negatively triggering
But I have heard that his promises bring about bigger things
Like living water that springs up in his sheep
And the meek - inheriting the earth
So I keep myself far away from myself first
Disarming the weapon that was born to this Earth
By filling myself with him first
And letting the Son shine brightening up what's dim

Letting me decrease so he can increase within
Bringing peace shutting all doors so that when I pray and release
it all goes to him
Transforming my bad to good - my dishonest to true
My will becomes aligned with you
Fully surrendered no triggers because God tells me when and how to move

<u>**Triggered**</u>
Living Word

"Disarming this weapon that was born to this Earth." Let's talk about that for a moment. If we know that we are born in sin and shaped in inequity, then why don't we believe we are our own triggers? Whether for the good of God or for the love of evil, we are born a weapon. We are born as a tool that is used to overcome or overpower something. The question is how do we pull our triggers and what do we aim at? It seems that more often we use our weapons for evil. We use our arms to throw punches instead of embracing. We use our words to curse instead of uplift and our eyes to lust instead of seeking. We use our feet to take us everywhere else but down the right path; and we use our time for ourselves instead of the building up of God's people. We have historically been our own worst enemy. There is nothing anyone can do to us to harm us more than we harm ourselves. This stems from our lack of honesty with ourselves. We call ourselves being "honest" with others but how can we begin to do that if honesty doesn't stop by your house first?

Being brutally honesty with one's self is necessary, we have to identify what's within first before we can identify afflictions or problems in others. The problem is, we most often choose to be double-minded or in other words have double standards when it comes to discerning and asking for a resolution for our problems. It's much easier to point them out in others. That's like casting a stone and shattering your own glass house because you are found guilty of the very thing you are judging others for.

Living in this world, many of us encounter people who cannot see themselves. They only see the version of themselves they create and present to others- the representative. The person we create to stand in place of who we really are, hiding our true nature. We call it an alter ego. A tailor made version of out self-esteem or self-importance displaying the life we want people to believe we lead and growth we want them to see in us.

Currently, we are living in a fantasy world of alter egos and desires that have been personified because instead of fixing a problem, people make it a trend. Now, instead of one doing a foul act, it's a community and a lifestyle that has been formed where people are okay with being blind to their own faults while pointing out the fault in others. We keep this going, generation after generation, until no one actually knows what right is anymore. Today's definition of "right" and acceptable is so steeped in the devil's weapon; over sexualized, violent, and blind that we just call it "the norm" and accept it even when deep down in our core we recognize that it's not of God.

This "norm" is formed because we call ourselves being triggered by situations that make us act on feelings and impulses. They react in what is essentially a knee jerk reaction, instead of looking within and being honest with themselves about why they are still holding on to that thing and seeking God for the remedy. Instead of saying, "Lord, this is still holding a space in my heart and it's eating me up", you weaponize your eternal emotions and lash out on others to make them feel as low or as angry as you're feeling now. Then after all of the damage is done, you say they triggered you, triggering the next person who then triggers the next and now that trigger is a norm.

Sometimes, triggers go deeper than hurt for the past or others and stems from vanity. Sometimes, it comes from thinking you can do no wrong, that we are always right, or always having a rebuttal because you feel your word is bond. This is especially ironic when your words are just really saying that you can't see past yourself and you are deflecting.

VANITY, which is an inflated pride in oneself can be the cause of your downfall. We all know pride goes before destruction making vanity a self-destructive weapon that is spreading like a virus, infecting all those who come in contact with it. I encourage you to read 2 Timothy chapter 3 to understand how in these last and evil days we act as the weapons. People who feel so entitled that they will cut you down just to gain something they don't even deserve; they are the weapon. The ones who will spread personal information about the action you were partaking in knowing they were doing them right along with you, they are the weapon. These kinds of people will over inflate their importance, they will walk around as if the world revolves around them and you are just taking up their space. They do this to make sure everyone around them feels small; they are the weapon.

Going back to the stones, in the Bible there was a woman about to be stoned for fornication and Jesus said, "he who is without sin among you cast the first stone" and today we are living in a time when stones are flying around everywhere like fiery darts because people refuse to receive the truth about themselves. No one even asked about the man she committed the sin with, they were just following the crowd in the uproar against the one person. This is an example of a trend. Not even the man involved stepped into say, "If you stone her, you stone me because I am to blame as well" likely because he didn't feel at fault. He couldn't see himself therefore neither could others. Even the multitudes there to stone were at some time or another guilty of a sin. As the Bible says, we all sin and fall short; yet it was a community of folk who were there to use their weapons for evil but not Jesus. Right there, He was the example of what it looks like to open the eyes of people with a good weapon, causing self-reflection. Turning the eye inward first before they have an outward response.

We pray for everyone and everything but never ask, "Lord where do I lack?" Let a man examine himself so that if we examine ourselves, we may not be judged. There needs to be a lot more self-reflection. It says, "…with love and kindness have I drawn you". We are not here to match energy, to match aggression, or to match wrongdoing with wrongdoing. We are here to shift the atmosphere and flip the script. We should be able to walk into any room and change the tone for the better. It doesn't matter the vibes or what spirit people give you or that they are operating in. What you give back is love and kindness because that is what's going to cause conviction. We are to keep our heart posture in line with the fruits of the spirit: love, joy, peace, patience, kindness, goodness, faithfulness, and self-control. That's the posture that impacts the flow of your life and others. Those are the weapons we need to use, the weapons of good to bring about life and not death.

We need to fine tune our weapons. 1 Corinthians 10 says, "Our weapons of warfare are not carnal but mighty in the pulling down of strongholds, casting down arguments, and every high thing that exalts itself against the knowledge of God; bringing every thought into captivity to the obedience of Christ and being ready to punish all disobedience when your obedience is fulfilled." Since we know we are the weapon we need to understand that our weapons aren't carnal, they aren't for physical use. When you throw that punch in the physical, you are now operating a deadly weapon and our weapon should bring about life. Hear me out, we are to pull and cast down (nondeadly) every high thing that exalts itself. We are supposed to knock those evil things off their pedestal and put them in their rightful position- low and under our feet. "Bringing every thought captive into the obedience of Christ" means your thoughts, your evil ways. Check yourself first. Being ready to punish all disobedience when your obedience is fulfilled- when you are honest with yourself, when you do away your own desires to exalt yourself higher than those around you... then you can utilize your weapon.

How are you supposed to identify a devil in someone else, when you haven't discerned your own? You are walking around with hate in your blood but telling others to love. The devil is not going to leave his position in your life willingly and that's why most of us can't see our faults because they are comfortable. Those poor habits become normal to you and that's how he tricks you into believing you are perfect and it's everyone else that has the problem. That is him using you to use your weapon in a deadly manner. When you disarm the evil within yourself, you're able to use your weapon properly and with love which brings about conviction which shifts the atmosphere. This nondeadly use of your weapon brings about change and newness in you as well as within others.

You have to realize that everything in this world is spiritual. Once you understand this fully, then you can load you weapon with the correct ammo and fight correctly. What comes out of the mouth is what the heart speaks and if it's postured in lust, then you're fighting on the wrong side of the battle. Our heart needs to be postured in the fruit of the spirit, the good ammo. You have to fight an opposing spirit with an opposing spirit because anger on anger will only equal rage. It's like trauma bonding in which you make a connection based on the wrongdoing that has occurred. When this connection is made, there is no change. The two just agree in the wrong name. You have to maintain an uplifting posture in both your mind and heart to win the battle. Fight depression with encouragement, fight lust with a positive outlet, fight fear with hope, fight death with life.

<u>Tug of War</u>
Spoken Word

A game we're all familiar with
Two teams standing on either side of the rope pulling until one side wins
It's usually a flag planted in the middle and you know the game is over
when one side slips
And the flag is pulled within the other team's territory - but here's my
story
I'm the flag tied in the middle of the rope
Opposite forces pulling me in two different directions - two ways to
cope
Holding on to the rope tight knowing the fight it's for my life
the winner - gets my soul
But the goal - that depends on me
With which side of my eyes today do I want to see
Do I want to be down with the devil or lift it up to another level
But still - I'm the flag from where I stand both sides look good given the
day
Or should I say depending on which way I operate
Both sides begin to pull and tug and as the flag I moved from side to
side
I feel the pull, the rock and the sway
From where I could be or where I can remain
From where I struggled or the solution I can gain
Truth is - the solution also depends on the day
Or should I say depending on which way I operate
Because the devil he doesn't come alone he brings his buddies
He brings who I am now and tells me its because of me
He pulls with guilt and with self pity
He pulls and he pulls and tells me you'll never make it to heaven – to
you it's a forbidden city

35

He pulls with the desires of the flesh he pulls and he pulls and he tests
the way I operate that day
Does depression look good to me today?
If so the table begins to tip and then I start to slip and to dip deeper into
his territory
But on the right I feel the fight that says cast your cares on me
It grabs my burdens and says you don't have to bare this – only me
And so I see this is not the side my flag should be
And then the light it starts to win and I begin to feel relief
I start to feel some strong belief
I start and begin to feel complete
And just then my friend comes over for drink and then I think
Well this could be fun - I can have just one and still remain in the
presence of the son
Until that drink turns into a bottle and then I watch and I follow my flag
Into the darkness - again
But the light doesn't give up doesn't give in
It pulls back on that rope tighter than before then begins
To show me living waters he begins to show me I can be one of his
daughters
Shows me that I have a choice if I speak and use my own voice
Shows me how to speak from the power within
Shows me where my life now begins
Shows me that he's the one with all the power
Shows me that he's this - strong tower
Shows me that he's this - light within the darkness
And it all starts with - him
That even in this game he already wins - victory
So you see - from the beginning the game was fixed
Even though for a moment when I was tormented within
The tables were turned switched in my favor but in his honor
The game was already won by the father

Tug of War
Living Word

The feeling of being pulled back and forth is our daily relationship with God. We are indeed the flag in the middle of this game of tug of war- opposing forces and emotions tugging at us daily causing an internal struggle. Some days, we wake up with our faith at a ten; while others, we wake up dragging our feet through the mud. Somedays, we wake up ready to face the world; while others, we bury out heads deeper under the covers snoozing the alarm clock. What happens if that day your alarm clock just stops, what side would you end up on? When we hear the trumpet sound and see God crack the sky, which side of the rope will you be on?

We tend to base our faith on how we feel on any given day. We base it on our emotions and that's a dangerous game to play. They can hinder the miracles we are scheduled to encounter each day and blind us from our path. Our emotions are roller coaster rides that take us up and down every single day- sometimes, several times a day. The thing is, while we're hitting those peaks and valleys, one false move could take us off the deep end or wrap us in bliss. Basing your faith on the instability of emotions shows that your foundation is not stable. Your faith should be unmovable, it should be sound. Fatih should dictate our feelings not the other way around because when we are rooted and grounded on an unchanging God whatever moves outside of our beliefs is not of God.

This got me thinking about the story of Elijah in 1 Kings chapter 17 through chapter 19. He was on an emotional roller coaster. A prophet standing on the word of God, who hears Him clearly and honors His word, goes into a depressed state wishing for God to take his life. When things were favorable, when it felt like he was on the winning side, he felt untouchable. Then opposition showed up and he feared for his life. When he challenged King Ahab the Bible says he taunted the followers of Baal to shout louder as they tried to call him down. So, we can say that he was feeling pretty good in his faith that day. When God was moving in his favor, hearing his voice, and bringing about victory, he felt untouchable; but as soon as the contest to determine the true God was settled, as soon as he put all the followers of Baal to death, he was met with opposition. Jezebel was threatening to kill him. From the high of winning to the depth of fear just that quickly. He ran into the wilderness, sat down under a broom bush tree, and prayed that the Lord take his life. He went from one extreme to the next; from taunting to throwing in the towel. From boldly announcing to the man killing his kind to cowering in fear. His faith was unstable. Just like Simone Peter who walked with Jesus performing miracles in His name. He went from witnessing crowds of people pushing to just get near them to denying His name as soon as the going got tough. When he had to stand amongst the same crowd and say, "I know that man", he denied Him. Both men went from one extreme to the other.

As the poem says, both sides look good depending on the way I operate that day. As the devil pulls on one side and God pulls on the other, we look at our situation. If we are feeling hopeful, we choose God; but if the devil shows up and casts enough uncertainty, we lean in favor of the doubt. The devil shows up to capture and accuse; let me explain. The devil will never show up with the chains that are used to bind us but he brings us choices. He brings us the links and makes us build the chains that we wrap around our own legs to keep us bound. Each link is presented in the form of something pleasing to us. Something that we would confuse for a blessing is truly a curse. Again, that lust of the flesh, lust of the eye, and the pride of life. He shows up with that women or man that's appealing to us or the social status we may have been yearning for. He shows up with that deal of a lifetime; but he never tell you that women or man is manipulative or abusive. He never tells you that social status bring enemies that will try to take your life to take your place; and he never tells you that deal of a lifetime will drain all the money that you have to your name.

We take the bait, we take the links and create the chains. Then once he has us on his side of the rope, he uses that same chain to keep you bound. Every time God pulls on that other side of the rope, he says, "Remember when you used to drink you have no place on that end of the rope. Your place is with me. Remember all those times you went home with anyone who would sleep with you, there is no place for a scandalous person on that side. Stay with me. You remember that time He gave you more than you could ever imagine but you squandered it He'll never provide for you again. As a matter of fact, He doesn't even want to see your face. You'll fit in better right here with all of the other outcasts." He sits back and dangles the very things that will keep us bound and watches us choose it every time.

On the other side of that rope is a mighty hand; stronger than any accusation held against you. On the other side of that rope pulls the conqueror who simply says, "Resist the devil and he shall flee from you, choose Me. I come that you might have life and that more abundantly. As far as the east is from the west I have removed your transgressions from you. I no longer hold you accountable for your past if you choose Me. If you choose life, I will blot out your transgressions for My own sake and remember them no more."

Elijah ran to the wildness and prayed for death. He fell subject to fear yet God continued to sustain him in his weak and vulnerable state because His power is made perfect in our weakness. Although Peter denied Him three times, He forgave him and reinstated him back into the rock that he was born to be. We serve a God that will not only forgive and forget but He will then lead and protect you. So, when you feel your life hanging in the balance, when your emotions are telling you that you are unworthy of being saved, when you feel like you're too ashamed to turn to God because of the devil's accusations… remember we serve a God that took on the weight of sin so that we wouldn't have to.

<u>**Free will**</u>
Spoken Word

Someone tell me how this will is free?
Please - make it make sense to me!
Your ways are not our ways and neither are your thoughts so I was
taught
Your ways are supposed to be freeing but what am I not seeing
Because everything I want to do seems to be in direct opposition of what
you want me to do
If anything it feels more caged to be saved
Feels like your will is always in direct opposition of what I have to say
Seem like your will only uncovers my rage so what's changed?
A slave to the world or a slave to your will it all sounds the same
My choices by you they are made so where is this free will you say?
To choose ye this day? that's the choice?
But where in this will is my voice?
All covered up under your word never to be heard what am I not seeing?
- until he showed me
Holy Spirit took me hand in hand and showed me the old me
Took me high up into his world hands in his looking down I didn't even
know me
He showed me a river and planted by it a dead tree
And he said that was me!
I didn't understand my mind began to fill with so many words so many
expressions
And before I could utter the words to even ask the question
He said this is you without divine intervention
This is you caged by a will of your own the will you choose when you
make this world your home

The will of your desires and your thoughts and in this will your life it
will cost
In this will your soul will be bound
Look at you – planted feet away from me yet still choosing to drown
How bound do you have to be standing feet from me and choose to be
this dead tree
You said make it make sense to me
I had to show you before you could know ME
Look deep into that river it runs deeper than you know
Swarming with living creatures and on the banks it overflowing
Spills over unto everything that's around
No other voice to be heard or to follow but my sound
You can choose to be this tree and I can say I know you not
Or you can lie in my will because and give real life a shot.

Free will
Living Word

Free will is often a hot topic when you speak to people who are still in and of the world. No one wants to be controlled by anything; no one wants to lose their voice or sense of self. Everyone wants to keep the control they believe they have over their lives. Yet, everyone wants call on the name of God when they are in trouble. People pick and choose when they want to call on His name or curse it because the same mouths screaming, "Lord save me" when they are in a tough situation, are the same mouths saying, "God knows my heart" when they party on Saturday and miss church on Sunday.

Our free will is in fact the choice to choose every day which you are going to serve- the will of God or the will of Sin. To been enslaved to sin or to be enslaved by God. That is the choice. I encourage you to grab your Bible and read Romans chapter 6 in its entirety as a reference for this part. You look at it we are a slave enslaved by something whether we are obeying our urges or we fight them, that is the difference.

To understand our free will, I believe we need to understand God's sovereignty which means He rules over all. He has all power and dominion. In other words, God's in control of all creation. It provides assurance that in following a just God, we can rest assured that everything has a plan and purpose according to His will. Since we are created in His image and likeness, we have the attributes of the Creator. While we can't create the path, we can alter it and this is where our free will comes in when we choose to deviate from the righteous path to the alternate.

Think about it this way, a car can't have two drivers. There's a driver and then there are passengers. You enter the car by choice, trusting that the driver will get you to your destination in one piece. Having faith that although you aren't behind the wheel, the driver knows what they're doing. Then we turn our attention to those backseat drivers, shouting instructions and criticism to the driver because they feel they know the best. We are living in a time of backseat drivers who won't release the control. Who feel they have to tell the manufacture how to operate the machinery He created Himself. If you want to choose to go your own way, then make the choice; but understand the consequences. Do you want to be a slave to sin or a slave to righteousness? You can't have both.

Sin and righteousness work in the same way, despite being opposite. It's the longevity that makes the difference. In sin, you experience what feels like a burst of life. Instant satisfaction. It feels like your heart's desires are being fulfilled because sin satisfies your flesh just for a moment. Sin is easy fun seeped in pleasurable moments that last just that, a moment; but this flesh has an expiration date. The lust of the world will die with the world. In God, the path feels like you're experiencing little deaths. You feel trials and moments that you would rather live without. This walk feels wrong. You wonder how could something hurt so bad but promise so many benefits? This world is not your home, so why lust to die when you could die to live?

Free will means when I choose to serve God, I choose to live according to His code of conduct. I choose to live an Evangelist lifestyle spreading the news as I go. Denying myself so that nothing is withheld from me. Being in the world but not of it. Hell has to be filled just as heaven does but it's not God's will for any to perish, that is your choice. We are predestined to be adopted as His sons and daughters through Jesus in accordance with His will. Understand what that means, we are not automatically His children; we are only automatically His creations. If you flip the verse, it says, in accordance with His will through Jesus Christ His sons and daughters are adopted and predestined. That means in order to be predestined, in order to reap the benefits of being saved by grace through faith - co-heirs with Christ, we have to live in accordance to His will. To whom much is given much is required. Do you think it's a small feet to be predestined to a royal family? Heaven is not first come first serve; its entry is based on who endures to the end. Who lives according to His will and His way. Freely following Christ is not a perfect journey, we are almost meant to fall because if we were perfect, we wouldn't need Him.

So, for the unbelievers, we are not living a perfect life we are just following a perfect God and striving to be like Him daily. Mistakes will be made but if you choose to remain in your sin, you will be like that dead tree. Feet away from Him yet choosing to drown because you want to be the lord and light of your own life. When you're in His will you won't feel like you don't have a choice, you won't feel like you don't have a voice, because they both will be aligned with Him if that's what you allow.

<u>**Overthinking**</u>
Spoken Word

What is my name?
is it what I call myself or is it my shame?
is it my blame? is it self-loathing?
for I am unknowing of the worth you find in me
this human being
this dirt with a life infused in it
this thing left unfinished
and I wish I knew me
the me you see with undoubting love and care
the image of you you see when in my eyes you stare
why can't I know it to be true?
why can't I see the me in you?
or the you and me giving lifeless words a reality
so speak that's the words I hear
there's power in your words wielded like a double edged spear
crossing out the words that bring about death because they're blotted from
the lambs book
and forgotten when the last breath you took
it's gone yet you hold on
because your name in my book next to it is written strong
it's chosen its friend it's child of God from the beginning to the end

<u>**Overthinking**</u>
Living Word

Attention all overthinkers, this one is for you. Attention all of the strong friends in the world, this one is for you also. What a lot of people don't understand is that overthinking and being the strong friend go hand in hand. I know this may sound contradicting but it will make sense after a while. Have you ever heard the saying, "check on your strong friends" and truly understood the reason behind it? If you are the strong friend, you understand that we put our needs last always acting in selflessness. We are the go-to person during rough season and often have the stamp of reliable on our foreheads. We carry the burden of others to lighten their load while making our own load heavier and although we suffer in silence we are often the cheerleader because we uplift others at all times. We could be overwhelmed or unsure and our worlds could be in shambles yet we have to stand firm for the people who are looking to us for assistance and guidance. The question is… who does the strong friend go to for advice? Who do they have in their corner to make sense of their own life once they find themselves buried at the bottom of the hardship pile.

Even though we wear our strength on our sleeve, like Samson, the job gets tiring and it leads us to overthinking. *Are You sure I'm called to help in this capacity? Who am I that You would entrust me to help these people? I have issues of my own that I am trying to balance along-side this! I have struggles of my own I need to overcome, yet You are calling me to led? Why can't I see the purpose, choose someone else this is too big for me! It's just a matter of time before I drop the ball because this weight, these bags that I carry on top of my own, is too much to bear. I can't possibly be cut out for this*! We have our days where we feel that we can't possibly be cut out for the job. That the strength that we are given is no match for the job God has assigned us; so, we begin to overthink and question our position. We question whether we are cut out for this because every day we feel one step closer to dropping all the bags and saying "enough!" At any minute we could be done with everything.

Moses is who comes to mind. He was born for his purpose yet he allowed himself to overthink. "God choose someone else I can't even speak correctly. Who is going to listen to me? These people won't follow me; I was once a part of the family that brought about their suffering. Why would they follow me? Who am I that I should go to Pharaoh and tell him tell him to let the children of Israel out of Egypt? God just send someone else!" We question who we are when who we are called to be is tough. When the road ahead is rough, we can't see how we are going to weather the storm. We don't feel prepared for the journey and we call out to God so that He can show us what He sees in us that we can't see in ourselves. Moses had many breakdowns before and after freeing the Israelites but the people never saw them. He always broke down behind closed doors with just him and God. When folk already feel they are in the midst of hardship, the last thing they want to see is the person labeled strong cracking. So, the strong friend I want to encourage to you take your frustrations to the Lord so that He can continue to equip you because it's not your strength you're operating on it's his.

If you feel that you are carrying the burden then here is the time as the strong friend to pass the burden along. While we bare the infirmities of the weak, we shouldn't hold on to them. We are to stand in that gap for them, we are to seek on behalf of those who can't. So, if you are heavy laden, lighten your load. The Bible says, "cast your care on him", that means the cares that you take on for others as well. You are the strong friend but you should have strong faith to match so that you stand in the gap as Moses did. He did not speak to the people without speaking to God first but the people spoke to him because they knew he could reach the throne, that is the strong friend. Say to them, "come to me because you know I can reach the man that will solve not only my own problems but yours as well". Teach them how to go to God on their own, creating more strong friends to help you carry the load. So that when you stand on the top of the hill with your hands lifted up, you now have a backing- a gathering of folk who will help you keep your hands lifted. People that will stand with you in the face of the enemy.

Strong friend, I want to encourage you to continue to be strong and courageous. Don't lose hope or be discouraged because God is with you wherever you go . Like Moses, He will provide you with all that you need to tackle the task at hand; be encouraged. Your strength comes from the Lord and He will uphold you in His right hand. Understand that you are made for this and on those days when you struggle to find the will to push through, when you struggle find the reason you were chosen for this, when you battle with the call that was placed on your life, remember that God give His biggest battles to His strongest warriors- mighty in His kingdom! Continue to come to the Lord in prayer asking not only for help for those in need but to renew your strength because if you are not good to yourself, you are no good for others. When you are faced with mountains, know that you have faith enough to make them move because your only option is to win. Even when you feel defeated, even when you feel you've lost sight of who you are as an individual, know that it's a trick of the enemy to get into your head and create doubt. To make you doubt your purpose, to make you doubt your strength, to make you doubt your connection to God to make you doubt the power that work within you.

Strong friend, I encourage you as you stand in the gap for others stand in the gap for yourself as well so that God can continue to renew your strength. So that He can provide you with a fresh wind daily. I want to encourage you that because your heart has remained in line with God, since you have continued to be a servant, whatever it is you need from Him, just ask. I pray that He fills you with the peace that surpasses all understand when you feel overwhelmed and that He continues to lead and guide you so that you can continue to lead His people to Him.

Not So Good Samaritan
Spoken Word

As I pull up to the building parked the car and before I head inside
I notice it's a rundown place where destruction lies
I can't help but feel those eyes watching from every side
My every step up the stairs into the hallway on the left
Past the blood stains on the chest of a man who chose death
Up another flight to the right stands a group of people
Full of lust and anger I could tell I could sense the danger
And the smell -a smell so foul you think how are they standing here?
In this stench by choice fists clenched drenched in the blood of the man
From the flight below
Yet I know I have to go no time for fear can't let that show
So I keep on pushing past the crowd and I can hear the voices speaking
And screaming so loud
Even though their lips don't move I can hear the sound
I can hear the torment I can hear their souls drown
But I keep on walking to complete the mission that was given in a vision
And in that instant on the wall it is written we all have sin and fallen
Short
But behind me I felt the opposition growing like a slow overflow from a
pot bubbling
Over and even though that sounds troubling
I know I'm almost there I see the door and I'm filled with peace that
replaces this despair
It swings open and as the hairs on my arms flares looking back at me in
A stare is a vision of the risen and just as plainly as I see I hear so clearly
-depart from me
You made it here but you don't have the heart of me
All at once my world is rock instantly my body shook as he looked past
me

And said you see those people on the stairs -you heard their pain but you
Left them there
The man on the steps who chose death he did it in my name
Yet you claim to be one of my sheep
But didn't utter a word to my people -not a peep
To those you heard weep yes you came to me but what's about the
others?
You walked right past your sisters and your brothers
Who were seeking shelter from their struggles lost
But yet their paths you crossed and turned up your nose because you
Assumed and supposed
They didn't want directions to the roads that led to me
I gave you the vision and yet you still can't see -blindly
I'm telling you and you still can't see I brought you to this place of
Destruction because you had their keys

<u>**Not So Good Samaritan**</u>
Living Word

Let's look at the story of the good Samaritan in order to understand the bad. The story in Luke 10:29-37 talks about a man going from Jerusalem to Jericho. He is attacked by robbers who strip and beat him. A priest and a Levite walk right pass him without lending a helping hand; but a Samaritan, his enemy, stops to help. He cares for him, takes him to an inn, and pays for his stay. Many of us feel that just because we seek God for ourselves, because we are on our own spiritual journey, we will make it into the kingdom of heaven without helping those in need. Matthew 22:37-39 says the greatest commandment is to love the Lord with all your heart, soul, and mind; but the second is to love your neighbor as yourself. Love is the foundation upon which God wants to us build. Not self-seeking, but to display love and kindness.

How many times do we overlook or ignore the transgressions of others just because we would rather not get involved? When we decide to live for Jesus, we are charged to help those who are in need. John 3:16, "God so loved the world that He gave His only begotten son that whosoever believes in Him shall not perish but have eternal life. "So that anyone who believes" means those who are in need that believe but don't know how to turn over a new leaf. It means those who have a heart for Christ but can't break the habits of the past. We are charged to extend our hand in help; to carry each other's burdens. We are not meant to do life alone, that is why we have brothers and sisters. So that when one falls, the body of Christ is there to lift. Matthew 25:35-46 I'll explain in my own words, but Jesus is calling those blessed to His right because when He was hungry, they gave Him something to eat. When He was thirsty something to drink, when He was a stranger they invited him in. When He was naked they clothed Him; sick, they cared for him, and imprisoned, they visited. They didn't know that this was the Lord in all of these instances, but they did these things anyway. Then Jesus replies, "Whatever you did for any brothers and sisters of Mine, you did for Me. Then He speaks of those on His left who are cursed because they saw someone in need and did not help. So, what is done to those in need, they have done to Him and will be eternally punished.

Sometimes, we are so caught up in our own journey and perception of where Christ is that we miss the fact that He is right in front of us. He's the group of people in the hall who look deranged but their soul is speaking His name. Those people who are homeless and hungry, who just need someone to give them change. The people in church who you count out because it appears their walk is different than yours but we are both walking to Christ. What's important is the fact that we are moving. Some of us feel they cannot stop and help others because they will be held back but if God placed people in front of you, it's for a reason. What if He just walked past the disciples in the midst of the storm as He walked on water. Yes, His path was unaffected but what if He totally ignored the disciples' need in the boat just because He was on his way to the other side with nothing holding Him back? We have to keep ourselves open so we don't miss Him on our journey. We have to understand that our instructions for ourselves will always include the helping of others.

Desert Season
Spoken Word

We only speak on a wilderness season but never the desert
deadly and uninhabitable
No water means no life like living a walking death - unimaginable
It's like a wilderness season but more perverse
Where death doesn't try to hide but it lurks
And your body is not only dry but it thirst
And your life not just a lie but its coerced
And how did we get so misplaced and displaced
Drought in our soul carrying sin and weights
Self-power we embraced
Sipping on water that was laced with disgrace
When we should be saved by grace through faith
But now we live in an atmosphere - a place
That's unsafe by mistake but is it a mistake truly?
It is us that choses to live a life that was unruly
Because when you know better you do better we've been charged to
accountability
We all sin and fall short and because we know that it's like we made it a
sport
We blurred the lines - distort saying things like we live a life that is short
So of course we will be dry bones sometimes
Sprinkled in the valley waiting for the prophet to prophesy
And to speak life into this dry spirit of mine
Waiting to be saved from these actions of mine
Waiting for the savior to save me from this pattern - my paradigm
And he's there just in the nick of time
He shows up then pulls me out but I jump back in stuck
And in the muck yet I'm waiting still for that spring of water to erupt
Waiting with my hands lifted up -fill my cup

Waiting for the blood to flow - cover up
Waiting for the mess I made to be cleared up
Waiting for the Lord to see there's some sort of mix up
But he says the mix up is the mix stuff you put in front of me
I said in my word all that thirst come after me
But you to yourself you became your own savior
And it's funny because you only come to me when you need favors
Then your favor you treat like a magic wand
And if even used like a wand you think you have to do my will for the
want to power on
Like it runs on your willpower instead of mine
And with this mind that's in you instead of the one that's in mine
You'll find yourself past the wilderness and in the desert every time

<u>Desert Season</u>
Living Word

A desert season is a walk through the wilderness without learning the lesson. Walking through, sightseeing, missing the point of the season. In the wilderness, you are being led through to the promised land or to the destination of God's choosing. When He is the pillar of clouds leading you by day and the fire by night. A place where even though you are disobedient, you are still within God's provision; He still hears your voice. He's raining down mana from the sky and bringing forth water from a rock when the cries of His people reach Him. When you are actively turning from your wicked ways it's just taking you longer than it should – that's a wilderness season. When you stop heeding His voice and step further and further away from Him, you're entering the desert season. Where there is no life, there are no provisions and the truth is distorted. You are seemingly on your own so far outside of the will of God it would take faith to move a mountain to change your situation. You would need that crazy faith to turn your situation around; but you can't seem to see yourself because in a desert, you start to hallucinate. You begin seeing mirages, seeing what it is you want to see. Viewing yourself in a different manner, thinking that someone or something other than yourself placed you in your current situation. Yet you are in that place where He has turned His face from you because chose to move past disobedience and into disrespect. When you move in His will just enough to get Him to turn the other cheek towards you, then grab your blessing and return to your wicked ways. A perverse way of life. When you treat your favor as if God is your own personal genie granting your every wish. Repenting just to get what you need and immediately reverting. That is a desert season.

What I've noticed is a lot of us don't even realize that we have entered the desert season because of entitlement… because of Inflated sense of self as if God is blessed when you speak to Him and not the other way around. You are standing in quicksand yet you're unaware because your perception of how low you are falling is distorted. Yet your view, both spiritually and physically, is so warped that you believe you are standing tall and strong. Maneuvering through life on your own time even upset because God doesn't move when you tell Him to. So out of reach you need to be taken to near death experience to snatch you from the fire. Allowing it to nearly consume you before you surrender. Living beyond the influence of flesh and into the realm of delusion. Disintegrating to the core and now you're only dry bones laying in the valley yearning for help but you are beyond the point of words. Unable to call out or speak a sound so you have to remain in that state, a mute state, until He decides to spare you or make you live in the reality you've created for yourself. Forcing you to suffer until He turns it around to work out for your good. Yet even in this state, you won't truly repent because you feel entitled. You feel that even if you are dry bones, He eventually has to turn your situation around because of His mercy. Allowing selfishness, pride, and inconsideration to become your down fall. Those are the spirits that kill you slowly. You don't even realized you are dying a slow death until the painful part hits. Until you realize that you are walking down a road by yourself and when you turn to God for help your words fall on death ears because through John 9:31 we know that God does not hear or entertain the prayers of a sinner unless it's the sinner's prayer for salvation. This is because a sinner will only pray in accordance with what they wish, again as if God is a genie. These are self-centered and self-serving prayers. These prayers skip steps in God's process almost stating, "Hey I know this is what you want me to do… but I don't want to and what I want you… have to give to me". How easily some forget He is a jealous God and when you enter the desert realm, you inter a selfish realm putting yourself higher than Him. Regarding Him only when you will it to happen, not operating in His will.

These are the people that are beyond the help of you and I. They need to a wake-up call and only God Himself can provide that. They are spiritually dead in their graves without the hope of escape until God provides a way of escape. Whether He shows them where this path will lead them in a dream or lets them sit in their own internal sorrows, only He can bring them back from the desert season. In Ezekiel 37, God asked, "Can these dry bones live?" Ezekiel replied, "Lord only you know, this is our place on the outside." Only God knows whether someone can be brought back from the desert season. Only when He decides to step into your grave, to step into the desert season and allow your bones to repent will you have a way out.

The bible said the bones replied our bones are dry, our hope is gone we are cut off. Given the chance to speak they repented. They used the opportunity in that desert season to say, "Lord I messed up! I went too far and now I'm without hope! I thirst, I'm all dried out. Please, I want to be back in your sight. This season where I am cut off from You can only end if You allow it.

When you feel you are beyond the point of no return, ask yourself can these dry bones live? Ask when they are reinstated to life, when I am allowed second wind, what will I do with it? Will I return to my arrogant ways where I see God as my employee, or will I serve with my entire heart? Will I know and accept that He is Lord? Understand that He is Lord and there is no life without Him. Learn in the season beyond the wilderness that you must give Him your undivided attention not the other way around.

<u>Notice of Eviction</u>
Spoken Word

Notice of eviction to my pain and suffering
Your reign in this jurisdiction has been replaced through this powerful covering
Grab a box and pack your things because here you can't reside
Pulled the blinds to the side, come on out, there's no place left for you to hide
Pull those shoes from under the bed because instead of your path that place has been filled
My steps are being ordered by him, quickening my strides - its time to rebuild
Take your toothbrush from the bathroom because it's full of curse words
It's time for me to speak those things that are not as though they were
Take that food out of the fridge because better food that I seek
I'm coming off the milk my spirit craves its spiritual meat
take your cup out of the sink because it's taking up space
It has to be removed to make a space for me to lay down my sin and weights
Leave your keys on the counter there's no way you can stay here
I've strayed from my path long too long and it's time this ends here
Living rent free in my mind because it's something I've allowed
And you've prowled -roamed free and it's me you disembowel
It's me you've torn to shreds filling my head with dread
When you misled me into thinking you and I were good friends
When I didn't know who I was, trapped In my feelings my emotions led me to you
And you greeted me with a smile and said my name is Pain how do you do
You said I know how you feel here's the deal and brought your buddy suffering

Now I regret opening that door because I was opening it up to other things
Like a gateway drug you showed me the ropes in hopes that I'd learn to cope
With impossible situations I know now I was not qualified to resolve on my own
They are out of my scope but catch this punch line - here's the joke
I'm putting back the pieces of myself that you broke
No longer fast asleep yes I'm wide awake - woke
Deciding to take on an easier and lighter yolk
So grab your coat and stay off my back I'm no longer in a state of lack
I'd rather sit at the foot of the table and accept fallen crumbs and to take a step back
In fact its time for you to exit there is nothing else to be said but to go back to where you came from
To those dry places I've now escaped no longer have to deal with he likes of this scum
So take everything that you came with I will not longer allow you to distract
Back to the atmosphere from which you came – that your home- now unpack

Notice of Eviction
Living Word

For every promise that you receive, there is a problem you are supposed to have a victory over. For everything living rent free in your head, for weapon that has formed against you, there is a victory to be won. These battles that we allow to live in our heads and in our lives we are supposed to serve them a notice of eviction. We are supposed to tell them they have no power, rule, or authority over our lives. We are supposed to conquer those things sent to attach themselves to us. The problem is, we learn to live with them instead of showing them the door. We allow them to come in and have a seat at the table God made in the presence of our enemy and destroy it. We allow them to come in and make a mockery of who we represent. These things that attach themselves to us need to be removed. How do you remove them? By using your words as a weapon and sealing it in the name of Jesus. Fighting with the tools Jesus used after He was tempted in the wilderness, "It is written". If being made man, Jesus was tempted and had to use the word as a weapon, why don't you think you have to?

In the beginning was the word, the word was God and the word was with God. So, the same word that spoke into existence can be used against things that exist in the world. Anxiety, it is written, do not be anxious about anything but in every situation, by pray in repetition, with thanksgiving present in your request to God and the peace of God which surpasses all understanding will guard your heart and mind. When you are brokenhearted, it is written the Lord is close to the brokenhearted and saves those who are crushed in spirit. When we are confused, it is written, For God is not the author of confusion but of peace. Instead of just allowing those things to operate through our vessels and break us down from the inside out, we have to do like our parents used to say- use our words. We have to bind, rebuke, cast out and then cover (in that order) those things that are not of God. If we bind and cover all we are doing is creating a wall around it and once it has broken free from its binds it remains. If we rebuke without binding, we enter into a fight; but once we come into the knowledge of Christ, we are no longer ignorant to the devil's devices. We can bind to stop it from prospering. We rebuke to remove its dominion or hold it has over us. Casting out to remove it from our bodies, homes, even our area code; sending it back to the atmosphere from which it came. Finally, covering ourselves in the blood of Jesus to prevent further attacks.

Listen, just because the devil, the unclean spirit, is cast out of the body doesn't mean the person is free forever. They are just free for the moment. They are empty or void of the spirit, evil or holy. This is why it's important to immediately invite the holy spirit to rest, rule, and abide within us to fill our house. We can sanction an eviction notice but we need to have a new tenant enter quickly. Matthew 12:44 the Bible says when an unclean spirit is cast out of a body it says, I will return to the house I left. When it finds the house, or the person, unoccupied it comes back with seven other spirits more wicked than itself to go and live there. Leaving the person worse off than when they first started. So, while we should always evict, we should also equip ourselves; they go hand in hand. Allowing ourselves the opportunity to experience full freedom from the unnatural wickedness living within. Receiving the holy spirit because that's where freedom exists- where God dwells.

Demons will conceal themselves, they won't reveal themselves or their motives until met with a higher or more powerful authority. Use not your name but in the name of Jesus where all power and authority lye. This is why the obstacles that are presenting themselves feel more extreme than what they are because they are unnatural forces working to overtake you. We have to look beyond what we see in the natural, this is why discerning spirits is so important. We have to have the scales removed from our eyes so that we can see the battle in the spirit realm. Ephesians 6:12 says, for we wrestle not against flesh and blook but against principalities, against powers, against rulers of the darkness of the world, against spiritual wickedness in high places. World. When we can see in the spirit realm, we can have the tools and weapons we need to expose the enemy that is coming to sift you as wheat. Without exposure, the enemy prowls around like a roaring lion seeking whom he may devour. He lurks and he lies to blind your eyes and he plays with your life by corrupting what we can see in the natural. Blinding us thinking like Samson, we won't call on our Father to help us take down the crowd. Reaching into our faith bag and pulling out that puzzle piece of faith that will complete the picture so you can see clearly.

While the attacks of the enemy seem unbearable, know that you are chosen because your name is a threat to the kingdom of darkness. If he's not bothering you, if he isn't trying to destroy you in any way, that means you are on his team. Why should he attack someone who is working for him, he already has you! When he chooses you to devour, that means you are doing what is right for the kingdom of heaven. It means you have the devil shaking in his boots and since he cannot stop God's will from coming to pass, he sets up detours. He tries to trip you up for as long as he can. A roaring lion, that means to, unless you relinquish the power, overpower you; but the devil is all talk and intimidation. It's us that provide him with the power to devour us. That's why you must fill yourself with the word so you have a powerful weapon to use when he speaks.

In the wild, when two alpha lions fight over territory, when they encounter each other, they roar back and forth to see who's sound is the biggest. Using its vocal cords to discern whether the lion on the opposite side has the power to overtake the area. The lion with the biggest roar typically scares the other away from the territory. Your mouth equipped with the word is your lions roar, sound it as a trumpet. Evict those emotions that have you stuck in bed watching the days pass you by, it's a trick of the enemy. Serve notice to that pain that had you pick up the pills and become an addict, expose the trick of the enemy. Walk your house and unlock the power because if he can walk to and fro, so can you. Devour the devil. Once you have reclaimed your territory, once it is swept clean, invite the spirit of God to make a home on the inside of you so you have a backing to resist the devil and he will flee in Jesus name.

<u>Constant Reminder</u>
Spoken Word

When you look at your life and see those places of desolation
those places that you felt were void of everything -empty and hollow
where the dark times seemed to find its home filling you with the
sensation of devastation deep down in your bone
in those moments when you hit rock bottom and you can't seem to get
any lower
and your cool is -lost lacking composure
and your mind is confused -you're not its owner
and you feel cut off from the world's -cold shoulder
remember God's got you
when in your days your reality is distorted by the emotions that you feel
that were left unsorted
and you can't deal with the pain that comes with living
and forgiving seems like it's the last thing you'll choose to do
when you perceive yourself through your own eyes through your own
lies the – the untrue
that seems to drive you off the deep end and suspends your will to go on
remember God's got you
when your life spins the track playing the same song on repeat
and those cycles keep spinning and spinning on beat
and winning seemed like it's seeped in defeat because your life is driving
itself
while you're buckled in the back seat because you allowed self deceit to
be the driver
here's a reminder God's got
you when your plan doesn't go as planned and you stand in the gap of
what you thought in actuality when what you plan to be would have
been an easier normality
than this insanity that is your life turned out to be
begins to feel like you're living in the danger zone -a walking casualty

but even when you feel you're living in a tragedy
God's got you
when your funds are running thin and you begin to feel pinned within
your circumstances
taking a firm stance in the middle of the hardship of poverty
Seeing the only delivery that arrives at your doorstep is misery to keep
you company
when instantly you feel the weight of your affliction
trying to ease the pain by falling subject to addiction
whether smoked, drank or by prescription
living life in direct contradiction instead of living a life led to fix it
just listen -God's got
when you feel your life beyond saving because inside you you feel a war
that is raging
and you feel it will bring about your demise
stuck up in the tower feeling like a damsel in disguise
like a wolf in sheep's clothing because even though it's the battle you're
exposing
it's you that's keeping it from closing
foot in the door keeping it going
fanning the fire and the flames acting in ways that are deranged
and knowing the fight is caused by you you feel the weight of the blame
thinking why would he even decide it's me he will to kick down the door
to save
when it's me that's putting those in danger - the others that he made
but yet when he showed up -when he came
He reached out his hand and called my name
even in my mess and my shame
no matter the situation the wage it's been paid
the facts still remains -God's got you

I was listening to this minister preach and his topic was so profound to me. He said, "I'm glad God didn't leave me where He found me." I started to think about how many times we have been in situations in our lives where if God didn't reach in and save us from our mindset or way of life, we would have allowed it to destroy us. If God didn't stop by and break up the relationship we had with the devil, if He would have just gotten there two seconds later in some stages in our lives, where would we be today? Then when He shows up, when He picks us up out of our mess, washes us clean, and says, "I will never leave you or forsake you, I got you. No matter how ashamed or embarrassed you might be, I see you through loving eyes. No matter what you've gotten yourself into, don't worry. I am here to get you out of it." Even while we are living a one track mind, stuck on destroying ourselves, He reminds us to let the mind be in you that was also in Christ Jesus.

I know there are times in our lives where we feel beyond cleaning, when we know the cause of situation is none other than ourselves, and we feel beyond saving. I am here to remind you that God's got you. This needs to be a constant reminder because we are always constantly sinning. We are constantly in a state of making the wrong choices that lead us down the path of destruction. Where our actions lead our emotions to feel that we just can't get anything right. I want to encourage you that God's got you. His love for us doesn't depend on our faithfulness, He knew we would choose the path of wrongdoing one time or another; but He loves us any how. His love is unconditional.

The story of the prodigal son is an example of His regard for us. In Luke 15, the father had two sons and the younger asked for his inheritance. So, the father split it between the two. The younger son went out into the world, spending frivolously, over indulging just living in the wilderness of the world. When a famine swept the country, and he began to live in a state of need and found a job feeding pigs. He grew hungry to the point that even the pigs' slop he longed to eat. The bible says when he came to his senses, he remembered how well his father's servants lived while he was starving to death and planned to beg for forgiveness from his father. He set off to his father's house and when his father saw him from far off, he was filled with compassion. He ran to his son and embraced him. The son began to apologize and explain that he was no longer worthy to be called his son but the father called his servants to bring his best robe. He planned a celebration for the return of the son. He said, "My son was dead and is alive again, lost and is now found."

When we become full of greed and overtaken by the lust of this world, we are driven away from our Father only to realize it was a temporary fix, temporary excitement. We live in this world and fall into relationships with it so deep that we forget the love and relationship we have with our Father. So, when we enter those moments of need, we still search to resolve our own problems and land in relationships that only drop you deeper into a state of lack. Where you are so hungry you'll eat anything, you'll do anything to survive in this world.

As the Bible says, we come to our senses. When we realize that we have to go back to our Father's house and beg for forgiveness. Yet even while repenting, like the prodigal son, we still feel unworthy. We still feel that we have fallen so far from the relationship we had with grace that there is no way we will be accepted or reinstated back into the position we once held. We believe we've caused so much damage that it's beyond repair; but God sees us a far off, He sees us in the mess that is our life and he runs to us meeting us where we are and embraces us. As we begin to beg for forgiveness and ask for mercy, He says, "My child who was once dead is now alive, once lost now found. I got you."

When we fall back into a relationship with Christ, He will always embrace us with loving arms because the child that turned from Him, the sheep that was once lost has found his way back to Him. The child that was once dead in sin is now alive through repentance. It doesn't matter what relationship or bond we have formed with the world, coming home means forsaking the world, no longer being of the world. Look at the things you hold dearest to your heart. Really dissect those relationships and should ask yourself, is it of Him or with the world?

The devil will come in and try to intercept your relationship with Christ and push you into relationship a with the world which he can manipulate. If he can introduce you to new relationships with him, if he can disrupt your bond with God and interlock you in relationship with the world, he can manipulate your broken state. In a broken state, you wouldn't make the same choices you would when you're in a whole state of life.

The relationship with money pushed the son into a relationship with greed which pushed him into relationship with selfishness and even into one with settling. Settling on the fact that if he went back home, he would live questioning whether or not he could be okay with living like a servant because he assumed that the relationship he once had with his father was no more. All of these decisions were made in broken states. When you are broken, you make broken choices and think broken thoughts. All you see is what went wrong but you don't see that God loves you anyhow. All you see is your fault in the matter but you don't realize that God's got you anyhow. You look at your situation and say, "Even if I return home, I could never be viewed the in same light as I was before I left. You can't see any amends being made because you are looking at life through a broken set of glasses but God sees you and runs to meet you. He comes to where you are and says, "Just because you started the path to me, I will meet you where you are because I know just making the choice to repair our relationship was hard. I see you in your broken stages before you make another broken choice to turn back. I'll come to you. I will meet you on the road that leads to me and make it all right. I will take you in the lowly mindset of eating the food of pigs, throw a celebration in your honor, and remind you that you are of a royal family. It doesn't matter what relationships you created in the world, what attachments they have on you still, I got you and all is well." We have to keep a constant reminder that it doesn't matter where we are in life, God's got us. 2 Corinthians 5:17 There for if any many be in Christ he is a new creature; old things are passed aways and behold all things have become new; Gods got you!

Joseph
Spoken Word

Fruit is always welcomed but no one wants to accept the pit
But to enjoy its sweetness we have to understand that the pit comes with
it
Understanding that the dark places we are planted
In the places that cause the most hurt, discomfort and damage
From the crushing in the darkness and the bruising in the hardships
The place where you feel you are struggling for air confined in those
places of despair
They Are all necessary, the crushing is necessary its for our good
So we should accept the pit
If you truly think about it the seed planted in the darkness gives it the
chance to submit
Gives it the chance to let go and allow the process to begin
To be placed in the fire and trust that what ever may come it will still
win
From the transition from a seed to fruit buried in a world of greed
Your seed was watered with positivity
That even when the fruit is ripe and ready to be picked
The Pit will remain – the experience will stay within
Whether an apple core, the seeds in a grape or the pit in a plum
They are a reminder of how your story begun
So even when you bloom from the tomb of your experiences
The Pit was a part of the process and serves as a reminder that you made
it
That's the pit within the fruits the hard truth within the sweet ending
The breaking down, the growing the shedding, the mending
The bending, the cracking, the blooming and the end products
Sprouting up from its roots when planted with a good heart are good
crops
But when watered with love in every raindrop
So we have to accept the pit we are placed in to grow

It's just a means to and end that we have to undergo
But remember the pit is not what's shown
Its just a personal reminder of how far we have grown.

Thinking of the life cycle, from seed into fruit. There are different types of seeds but they all consist of three main parts, the seed coat, embryo, and its food. The seed coats cover the embryo and keep it from drying out. It's also used to sense when the seed is in the right place to start growing. If the seed is not in the right place to start growing it lies dormant or in a state where it's alive but its inactive, slowed down for a period. The seed will remain in that state until it's planted in the right environment which has a balance of water, temperature, and light. Once planted in the proper environment and conditions, the seed coat lets water inside and the embryo feeds on the water and plant food provided in the see covering. Once the embryo inside the seed covering beings to grow, its roots crack the seed covering first. The root, no matter which way it's planted, knows which direction down is and journeys in that direction until it reaches a solid surface. Once it finds solid ground, this prevents the plant from falling over or being blown away; it keeps it stable.

As the plant grows some more, the stem cracks the seed coat again pushing its way to the surface until it sprouts above ground. At this stage, it's able to draw its nutrients directly from the light source and continue growing until it creates fruits and seed of its own.

I know that was a long description of the lifecycle of a seed but it's not without purpose. We are the embryo while God acts as the seed coat. In those stages in life when it's time to grow, He covers and protects us from dangers seen and unseen. He takes us and places us in the perfect environment for us to grow. Most times, where He places us looks unfavorable because just like a seed goes into a dark hole, so do we. Although you wonder, how would anyone grow in this situation, God hand-picked each of our holes and knows that it will provide us with the perfect conditions.

As we feed on the food and water, or the bread of life and living water that He provides us in our covering, we being to expand and eventually we begin to outgrown our situation. Our roots break the shell first and since we were watered in Jesus, our foundation will be rooted and grounded in Him. After our roots take root, we undergo another growing and our stems break through causing us to raise our hands to God. Now that we are grounded, we can seek Him, we can bask in His sunlight. We can venture out into the world knowing that we have an unwavering foundation. Knowing that when the storms come, we are secured in place. Then as we reach our peak of growth, our fruits show and can be picked and used for God's purpose. Fully ripe and ready to be utilized for His glory.

We have to remember the pit, the place we were planted, was to develop us into our purpose. We had to be shielded and watered by God in order for our roots to be rooted and grounded in Him. Once we are rooted and grounded, we are able to emerge from the darkness of the pit into the light of the world.

We all must start small, like a seed, and grow into our purposeful fruit but that growth is never without hardships. A seed cannot avoid being buried nor the cracking of the see coat - the breaking down of what it started off as to transform it into what it was meant to be. Just think back to a time you started anything, was it ever easy? Was there ever a time something of purpose came without a season of darkness?

The story of Joseph starting in Genesis 39-45, he was given a special coat of many colors and was disliked by his brothers for being a dreamer. They wanted to kill him but stripped him of his coat and threw him in a pit instead. Shortly after they saw travelers and sold him as a slave. In his time enslaved, he was given favor and worked for pharaoh who put him in charge of his house and everything he owned. Then he was accused of sleeping with his owner's wife and thrown into prison. Even in prison, he received favor and the guard placed him in charge of the prisoners. Eventually, he was released for interpreting the Pharaoh's dreams, given another high position, and showed mercy to his family when they came seeking food. Even in his encounter with his family, his brother didn't recognize him. He did not favor the boy they thew in the pit because the pit changes you. Jospeh was no longer the seed covered in the coat of many colors his father gave him; he was the product of the seed that was thrown into the darkness of the pit- covered by God's grace in his journey that resulted in the fruit of giving as he showed mercy on his family. Those dark places, those pit places, those places you see as the end… those are in fact the end for the seed but just the beginning of the fruit.

<u>Living word- I Hear You Always</u>
Spoken Word

I thank you for you hear me always
Not just sometimes but always
So when I'm all the way in my mess
When I almost did my best
When I did less than live a life that's blessed
I thank you for you hear me always
Even in my darkest hour when I've thrown my own hands up and say
hat's it
I can't help but reminisce
On the countless time you've wiped my slate clear – court adjourned
case dismissed
I thank you for you hear me always
I know I complain and live life of self gain
And sometimes my action are no less than insane
Same actions expecting different results – unsound mind
But in the depths of my heart Its your name I find
Written on its walls waiting for my call like I take no blame no fault at
all
I thank you because you hear me always
Even when I change living in my own lane you remain the same
Like a bridge built to last standing on the solid foundation the
Cornerstone of my life my rock and my savior
You remind me that you're the chain breaker
And I thank you for you hear me always
No matter the situation you hear me always
Just when I think I'm unheard I hear the words
I hear you always

<u>Living word- I Hear You Always</u>
Spoken Word

God hears you always. Even in the raising of Lazarus, Jesus thanked God because He hears him always. Sometimes we just have to thank Him for His listening ear. Reflecting on times in our lives when we thought our voice was beyond His reach, He still heard us. In those times where we couldn't even utter a word, we just groaned in pain, the Bible says, God hears the groanings of His people. He hears the cry from our spirit. Remaining thankful is powerful. The Bible says, in all things give thanks. So, I thank you lord for being in the midst of all my endeavors. That when I couldn't pick myself up you lifted me from a place of torment to a place of peace. That even in the moments in life when my faith wavered, even when my heart was broken what I thought was beyond repair, You are near to the brokenhearted. In the darkest moments, when my flesh wanted to turn from You, when in my heart I felt the darkness trying to overtake, You created in me a clean heart. When I hit rock bottom, when the ground I stood on wasn't stable, You placed my feet on to solid ground. You filled me with living waters that have sprung up and runs over onto everything that I touch. Giving me the victory, giving all who accept Your living waters the victory. Anointing my head with oil so now everything I touch has a touch of You.

I thank You for standing with me in the fiery furnace. I thank You that even when my enemies sought to turn it up seven times higher, not a hair on my body was singed or the smell of smoke present. I thank You for choosing me to be a living testimony so that I can lead others to You. I thank You that when I show up, You show up with me; and that when I am too weak to show up, You show up on my behalf. Forcing those I encounter to meet the One who saved my life. To meet the One that I honor all the days of my life.

I want to be like Mary, who wanted nothing from you but to sit in your presence. I want to pour my valuable perfume on Your feet and sing praises to You for blessing me. To give the little I have to You for opening a window of heaven and pouring out a blessing that I have no room to receive. For the word exceedingly and abundantly above all I can ever ask that You provide me. For the readers, under the sound of my voice, I want to thank You in advance for them receiving Your living word. Thanking You for the hearts what will be touched in my sharing. Thanking You for the conversations that will begin even without me knowing; but known unto you, that this book will draw all people unto You. That those who are drawn to You will draw more. That the community in Christ will be the only community known in all the Earth. That all honor and glory goes to You and that each reader will shout from the mountain tops the good news of Jesus.

I thank You in advance for opening up their understanding to receive all they have read and to add revelation upon revelation as they go deeper into Your word. That as they read they venture out and seek You all the more. That You touch their hearts in a way that they have been looking for all their lives. That You bring about a peace and a stillness where they know that it can only be You. That when they venture out into the word they hear Your voice in the stillness of the wind and the chaos of the storm. That in their everyday journeys, they remember to live their lives to end in the path that leads to You. That in all their getting, they get and understand a relationship of their own with You. I thank You because You hear us, not just myself, always. It's these things I pray. Amen.